take me for tame

Shoshanna Rockman

take me for tame

Dedicated to my children

take me for tame
ISBN 978 1 76109 614 3
Copyright © text Shoshanna Rockman 2023
Cover design: Olivia Smyth

First published 2023 by
Ginninderra Press
PO Box 3461 Port Adelaide 5015
www.ginninderrapress.com.au

Contents

Foreword	7
Between	9
The original	13
Children('s) (court)caught	14
No more poetry	16
Dementia is preferable	17
Paddington Bear – *I empathise*	19
72 kg	20
In public	21
The sober hook-up	23
Old One Eye	24
The word *ecosystem* seeped into my head	26
Wadawurrung Country	27
Compliments	28
The Locksmith	30
Bear country	32
Piano man	33
I tip them into boxes	34
Comfort zone	36
The beginning of love is hardly the challenge	37
The sharing of love	38
MY EX HAD A BABY – with someone else	39
Blame	41
Penetrate	42
Cleanliness is next to godliness – for some	44
Totemism	48
Package deal	49
Pattern making	50
Settlement	51

Pure poet	52
The truth about my WRITING	53
I so admire Medusa	54
Cup of grit	55
The resurrection of the black banana	56
The hawk and the tripper	58
Assertive	59
Dragons don't smoke	60
Acknowledgements	61

Foreword

A reading

I read my poem to resounding silence. Then I know why it is I write – towards spaces, crevices and gulfs. Towards figuring living. A summation of ghosts.

What we intuit between the lines allows the dragon to breathe its purple fumes, abandon its cave and – eventually, maybe – even put out the cigarette. (See 'Dragons don't smoke'.)

Between

First generation

YOU SPOKE Yiddish, Polish, German, Russian,
disparate dialects of English – broken
and cobbled together in the kitchen, amid fronds
of dill and sizzling onions.

When your own language reads from right to left
and your tongue and heart belong a hemisphere over,
the world tilts at dizzying angles. To learn English
in your middle years

when you worried about food and roofs. Your instincts
still bent towards survival – because you knew guns
and bombs, and snowy streets without jacket or shoes.
You were pried from school,

kept from polishing your own tongue
in your own birthplace. You did not learn the secrets
of burial. I learnt to converse in Yiddish. To read it too.
But you flipped to Polish and left me behind.

Second generation

A double identity can feel like none at all. We – or no one.
And it goes on. Because Holocaust survivors continue
to survive – and safety has no bearing in the aftermath
of smoke. My mother grew up

in too-long shadows of those walls, with all that soot
still flying in her eyes. And they wanted to protect her –
always. Which is why they made sure she studied hard,
completed high school,

went on to university. To become a doctor upon sound advice.
Some pressure. Which is partly why her marriage to my father
fell into so much rubble. The glitter of guilt never far behind.
After all, she was beholden –

Third generation

I have relatives flung wide in the aftermath of war,
family in Israel too – Hebrew, a second fork in my tongue.
Not whole enough for the צברה, the local, who mocks
my status as תיירת. My מבטא.

My fair skin. And hair. They are suspicious of me on the street,
and when I try to enter Synagogue, I'm to show my passport.
I switch to Hebrew. Try Yiddish. Begin to trace my family tree
in the dust at their feet.

Back in Melbourne, I'm still in between. I lurch from
my English name, Sharon, to my Hebrew, שושנה – and back.
So often, I can't be bothered with the stutters, the mash
of sounds. The querulous status quo.

And I'm between pages, which follows on from history,
ensures I remember my roots, my refugee standing. My family
who fled. My parents who live hemispheres apart – same city.
But without a common tongue.

Fourth Generation

I marry – deep into the fold. We build a house. Move on.
Move in. Build a double-storey, which crumbles
into debris. Into divorce. Afterwards, I move between houses
so the children can stay put.

The original

My parents divorced when I was 8 months old.
They took advantage of the Family Law Act,

the no fault clause – its ink still wet in 1975.
Of course the faults were still felt,

but they didn't need proving – or judging.
Well, not by a judge. Both went on to remarry.

Both entered new newnesses, new houses –
new spouses and newly conceived newborns.

Two new lives. Two new nuclei that I floated
between, that I tethered and tangled through

my ages, ancient histories and anarchies.
My half-siblings on both sides grew

to love me and miss me when I moved on
to other houses – leaving them suburbs

and eons behind. As though I were exulting
in some empyrean off-limits to all but me –

the half-breed. Which is how I came to terms
with my floating tenancy – with myself.

Until yesterday, when a childhood friend asked
had I never realised that I was the original –

of the original union. The one and only
fossilised solo. Bathed alone – in full-blood.

Children('s) (court)caught

I remember those ghost(s)/ly
white lights.

The chill and garish hues of the playroom
where we children skulked when our parents
departed to f(r)ight in civility and(/that) suits (–)/in
hushed tones and carpeted rooms.
      I remember *Romper Room* blaring
while I fretted. Anticipated my (twisted) turn.
It was like some spoof, a forged Gan Eden –
all the latest toys I'd seen on repeated ads
splicing the morning cartoons I loved so much.
Those smiling (care)free TV kids who played –
no palpitations, just children.

And our super(spectre)visor floated among us
with her phantom cheer and somnambulistic smiles.
Advocating toys and flinty games as saviours.
      I pitied her aimlessness. Her unknowing.
Her need of reassurance – that she was real
and exist/(exert)ing (some influence over us children).
So I conceded to play with the pop-up treehouse
that must have been expensive –
and still had all its coloured entrails intact.

A black(ened) suit and clipboard came to collar me,
    and I was/seemed obedience – along a tunnel
that led to a chamber/(steel trap),
where I was politely instructed to sit between
parents – commit treason against each one
in turn. Before court officials
who grilled, (s)tabbed – and notated.

I (took) refu s/(ge)/ed (in) the game plan –
the one remaining,
the one devised well in advance,
the one I'd sworn to follow.

Silence. My only (move)
weapon.

No more poetry

He talks about his ex's pathology, Her games. I baulk at the whip
of words, the lash of terms. The stream of key dates, adjourn-

ments, mediations, Child Protection intervention, AVOs and ABCs
of parenting – all misspelt, he says, by a sanitised system unused

to male victims of family violence. It can barely accommodate
the stock-standard DV, IVOs, 000s, burdened DHS. And NTV

(no to violence) incorporates the MRS (Men's Referral Service)
and MBCP. In fact, no Female Behaviour Change Program exists.

I see how he suffers, how he puts working – and living – on hold.
How he fights to see his kids. To be a parent. The proceedings

are all he has. I hear the accusations. I know the beer. The endless
cigarettes. The bare walls. The waning funds and hopes. The waste

of years. And my story. It's a rivet in the same machine. He's part-
gracious, part-sympathetic, part-furious at my femaleness –

my failure to calibrate this system. His internals rust. He's brittle.
Rebukes me for writing poetry, which has no structure after all.

Dementia is preferable

(not after my mother)

It started subtle. Trundled tortoise-like. Forwards.
Troubled by her mobile, mobility and mood.

Then time of day. And date. Then era. Her inability
to cook or hook her bra. Those free-flung breasts.

And jumbled limbs. The unwashed smell – of her.
Words in riot. Their random order. Skewed syntax –

too inventive – too new for growing older.
Her memory like soft sepia photographs,

those loose in shoeboxes that don't merit albums.
Disinterest in all the interests she'd had before.

Passed from gp to geriatrician to geriatric psych.
Unhanded at the memory clinic. I lug her in –

stumbling upon flimsy protestations. An MMSE
assessment – a practical tool for those whom

practicality has abandoned. By degrees. Or long leaps.
To grade cognitive skills. Or remnants –

1. Orientation 2. Registration 3. Attention
and Calculation 4. Language

Of course, she could not manage alone. Stashed
in a home. A locked wing. She didn't whine, writhe

or croak – after that. I visited – on occasion.
She slumped submissive. Demure. Accepted dry kisses.

Crumbs. I gloated. Grateful and blessed I had her.
Finally. The mother I'd always wanted.

Paddington Bear – *I empathise*

The label around his neck reads –
Please look after this bear.
The instructions for looking after me
were inked directly onto furlessness –
and there was no *Please*.
Just my name, phone number and address. Since I
was too small to be trusted with commitment –
of details etched upon memory. But not too small
to be misplaced. Mislaid. Not too small for instruction.
What to do in the (un)likely event –
*Find some nice lady, or a man in uniform. Show them
your arm. You know – the ropes.*

I got to know the rough fibres, the twist
of empty space
that would unravel by my side – amid the throng
and knots of full bodies at the market. The showground.
The shopping centre. The longer I was stoical,
the longer I remained alone. So I learnt to cave and cry,
to untwine in some ugly little office space with strangers
who commanded airwaves – used the PA
to broadcast
a call to the owner(s).

72 kg

My eldest leaped centre stage –
between the island bench and our table.
I'm huge now. I weigh 72 kg he said.

I reeled back to my arrival
at the hospital doors, already pleading
for an epidural. My weight, when

they checked it – 72 kg. Full of him.
His foetal peak. His accomplishment.
He dwindled upon cordlessness

to a still-impressive 4.2 kg, and I too,
dwindled without him. Without
all that flesh and fluid he'd added on.

I lost the great balloon of myself. Heard
the hiss. Punctured like a pool toy, I shrunk
into something soft and misshapen. Lacking.

In public

It was all green and blue and yellow.

I was hot and tired and overwhelmed.
Seven bickering children. All in need
of lotion, goggles – instant icy poles.

Endless Vegemite sandwiches – or jam.
Cut fruit and quarter-hourly toilet breaks.
We spread our towels by the pool
but the squabbles escalated. I tried. Failed.
Tried again for quiet. And the woman, one

towel over, glared at me over the head
of her toddler. Her displeasure
at the noise. At my lack of control –
or my abundance. I redoubled my efforts.
Tripled them – gave it up. She shouted.
This time, I shouted too – that the pool
was public. That I was doing my best

work. She yelled something about

the angelic qualities of her boy. I might
have yelled back that he was still small –
and had no rivals. She hurled another insult

while I wilted – and then the pause.
And on the brink of that, my eldest son,
about nine, turned. Suggested she
move. Told her to mind her own business
too. Another pause. Laden. My conscience

coiled. She sprang up – red and roiling.
Demanded I deal in discipline –
dole it out. I mused a moment. Looked
at my boy. Announced – in fact
he was right. He looked. At me. And saw.
The kids were amiable and easy –
all afternoon.

The sober hook-up

Hey, Mum, he drawled as he swung into the kitchen around noon. *My mates got so drunk last night – wasn't fun. They were dodging cars and yelling in the street. The girls lifting their tops for passing motorists – and no one was making any interaction count.* I took in his Tarzan frame, coffee skin, worried velvet eyes. I worried

too of course. I'd been warned by other mothers. Other women. And men. Unmasked-for advice about curtailment. Might call it envy. Or fear. Some of it well-meaning – about my onus and duty. His looks. A lot to manage – for him, I mean. The projections of others. Prejudice the danger. *So that girl I mentioned, the one who's been flirting with me –*

she asked to hook up last night. I interjected, *And then what? Well, I told her to sober up. I said she couldn't possibly know what she wanted. Asked her to call me tomorrow. I really am keen, you know. But I just couldn't make a move. Not with her so wobbly.* I stopped him. *I'm proud*, I said. *What for?* he asked. Impatient. *Hope she calls.*

Old One Eye

(after Jack London and my second son)

The old wolf is titular. But I focus
on my son. At fifteen, he still loves
being read to out loud. We begin –
a cushion apart. Steal closer. Classic
tales of the natural world. Better yet
if they contain icy peaks, gale force winds –
and wildness. Best
if they contain wilfulness
and wolves.

He has the flu when we read *White Fang*,
droops but urges me on and on –
and on over mountains which I scale
because who knows how far, how long
this close adventure will last – before
the girlfriends intervene. The pride
the parties –
the inevitable divide.

So I forge ahead –
through escarpments, caves, ravines,
through jack pines and larch bowed
by heavy drifts, and ice melting brown
between rocky outcrops – until he drifts
too. Then startles. Awake.
Asks what happened – to Old One Eye,
that scarred warrior who succumbed
to a she-lynx some pages back.
And, in the last paragraph, the last cub
was almost eaten – when a wolverine
invaded their den.

And One Eye's demise had nothing
to do with wolfish vision, impaired
or otherwise. And everything to do
with regeneration – with cycles.

Perhaps he hadn't fallen
asleep, my boy. Just verging
on his own –
wilderness.

The word *ecosystem* seeped into my head

THERE ARE THREE small girls, two larger boys, and a mum – bare-limbed, brown-skinned and salted. In the Torquay outskirts, we wander through wetlands, where a river snakes beyond houses. The scrub teems with Aussie browns and grey expanses of mud, whose acrid scents and textures squelch promises of dirt and diversion. There are also shell shards, and whole perfect ovals and spirals, with smooth cream interiors – or gaudy mother-of-pearl. And, there are in the banks, endless burrows for the carapaced and clawed. The brackish waters winch into clean cobalt waves, as silence builds to thunder. I grasp my girls' hands and we look around for the boys. Vanished. Nowhere on ochre sands. They must be left behind in mud. We retrace and find them digging for crabs with a group of younger kids, who have buckets, eskies and tongs. I think to yell at my boys – but then I see how they're helping the little ones who are scared of the pincers, and it's only my boys who bleed as they scoop and fling cantankerous crabs into the esky – until its full. Until the lid won't shut because the mass that moves inside is piled so high.

Wadawurrung Country

WE CALL THIS coastal town home. We've owned the ocean views.
    But now we cinch our belts tighter, breathe in – deep.

It's not for the sea breeze, infused with flotsam, dead things
    and so much dust. It's for the space. So that we occupy less
of it, as new suburbs encroach on steel legs, flat cement feet
    and a surplus of nails. We shudder as they tramp
across farms, fields, across wetlands – right up to the brink.

    We shrink and shirk. All that self-pity, pitted outwards against
government and industry – those who made us, built us up
    from yellow sand. But now our doorsteps crack and crumble,
we think in concentric circles, circling all we have and took

    – and lose. We drill down. Our flat rooves. Wide balconies.
Second storeys. The foundations forged upon originals and firsts.

Compliments

1.

I was of that vulnerable age, or stage,
when compliments count – are meaningful
and full of matter. You perform. To extract
them from peers, crushes, teachers –
from parents. I wasn't good at the game. Didn't
wear the right clothes, get in with the right crowd,
compete, curse, cave or crave – the right stuff.
Could never stand to wait it out, wait my turn,
turn somersaults for gain. Oh sure, I wanted
an A in English – also, I wanted to survive.
So I opted out of the clamour and clash –
the jostle for prime position
in that queue. I had to hunt a different way,
find a point of entry beyond crowd pleasing –
and just around crags.

2.

I took my bluey to the vet.
The old Scot with zero bedside manner
but some 30 years' experience – in the outback
and on farms. A specialty in bull health. Multiple
accolades from WPSA, RSPCA and AVA.
Now this plodding suburban gig. I respected
the science, the medicine, the attitude –
the almost wolfish ego.

Caulfield clinic. The waiting room full –
groodle, schnoodle, labradoodle, cavoodle,
spoodle, retriever and cat (Persian).
My grumpy rescue heeler-cross was not at home,
not amenable to pats or treats or trickery. A dog
who wouldn't wag, grovel, fawn or cower.
Certainly, no licks on offer.

I was primed for impatience. A tougher job
for the vet. In the exam room, I gave my dog
that look, a slight nod in his direction to convey
my expectations, my presence and my honourable
intentions for his best interests and care –
despite the needles, the wicked waft of disinfectant.
The looming stranger.
I told the vet – straight up. That my dog
would very much like to bite him – and hard.
But gave my word he wouldn't.

And the vet slowed. Checked my mongrel over.
Diagnosed osteoarthritis. Folded thick matted
arms. Leant back against the wall. And pulled
off his gloves. An inscrutable smile. A hot
meaty sigh. He complimented the both of us
on a dog–owner bond such as he hadn't seen
the likes of. In ages. I'd achieved my A –
in Affinity. And the acknowledgement –
of my primal position.

The Locksmith

There is something secret
and mysterious about keys.
– Deborah Levy

And that something is some
feat of mechanics, something
kinetic at play

inside a pressed rectangular
slab of wood. Some complex
iron system

of minuscule moving parts, in
which something turns, shifts
and slides.

And you wield that instrument
to come, go, enter, exit, lock
and unlock.

There is something singular
about that unexpected gust.
That determined

slam. It's cold outside. You call
the locksmith. Late. Somewhat
desperate.

Less than a minute –
a swift swipe of his palm-sized
white plastic gadget

down the jamb and it all swings
wide and vulgar. He is sure to
remind you –

a locksmith never needs a key –
any formal invitation or consent.
Written or otherwise.

Bear country

Bear spray. I didn't believe it either. I laughed out loud. My friend
– an engineering, mechanical sort – mentioned it apropos
a recent security breach. Of my home and self. He consoled me

via an anti-bear formula. He'd seen it himself in Walmart, Costco
Supercentre and Family Dollar, atop mountains – of Montana.
Turns out a grad student, Carrie Hunt, founded Counter Assault in the 80s.

The super-powered aerosol boasts a spray range of over nine metres,
a spray time of seven seconds. Effective against charging bears.
Smith et al. found that bear spray stopped bears' *undesirable behaviour*

in 92% of cases.* Of course, bear spray is no substitute for proper bear
avoidance strategies. Travelling and camping with common sense
remains recommended for managing ongoing human–bear conflict.

Bear spray is legal across the United States. In Canada, while lawful
for use against bears, it is prohibited as a management strategy
for humans. But I've heard of no such injunction – in Australia.

---

* Smith, Tom S. et al. (2008). 'Efficacy of Bear Deterrent Spray in Alaska' (PDF). *The Journal of Wildlife Management.* 72 (3): 640–645. doi:10.2193/2006-452. S2CID 24067944. Archived from the original PDF) on 26 December, 2011. Retrieved 27 March 2012.

Piano man

I didn't ask
for your song.

I tip them into boxes

There's something about a torso wrapped in thick
black leather under heavy rain that makes betrayal
easier to bear.

As if the pounding does not penetrate, as if patterns
can be undone – easy as a half-made sleeve
unravelled by a kitten.

A loose strand suggests a long and vivid invitation
to join some game, perhaps an exasperated sigh
countered by love.

And my friend of thirty odd years – he knows me
well enough to know the furrows that I've followed.
And those ruts.

He's heard me say it – I won't step in that vicinity again
because I've changed my feet, my gait, my landscape.
My tools of navigation.

I've tossed the old aside. He knows all this but wants me
backwards, which isn't a friendship thing to do or want
for anyone

let alone someone he professes to care about. Love
and let go. Leave be, when your own wife calls,
when you know about the box

I've stashed predation in – to prove that cardboard walls
can be built of stone. Stoical and heartless.
He pleaded with me

not to store him there in darkness. But I remembered how the last one begged the same – his predecessors too. A growing collection.

Comfort zone

I'm curious about this comfort zone
they speak of, are drawn towards, worship even.
When told I'm brave for veering from it, I nod
my head, pretend to know, try to feel
its contours in the dark. I want to believe in
what they cherish – and guard so close. I figure
it's some sacred space inside a circle
that some sorceress has outlined in chalk,
within which nothing loud or bad or frightening
ever happens – or is never sanctioned as such.

I'm curious about this comfort zone.
This exclusive club, the price of membership
and ongoing clamour –
its jurisdiction. Sometimes, I peer
over the white line. And sometimes I feel
lonely. Singular beyond containment. But mostly
I think about unleashing
a poem that delivers a swift and potent punch,
knocks me to ground, only to haul me up –
with a smooth slim arm.

The beginning of love is hardly the challenge

which is why we use sticky terms
    like honeymoon and sweetheart
whilst gifting chocolates

and eating ice cream midwinter.
    We dream faith into thin adhesives
while gliding serene with skates

laced high and white around ankles
    because drifts accumulate this season
which is ok. It's how you somersault,

how you maintain a mutual balance
    as the world underfoot tilts,
melts and refreezes.

The sharing of love

It seems natural to me
that sharing bodily fluids
leads inexorably and directly
to the sharing of pizza.

But a friend told me
otherwise –
a lunch date in sunlight
with a beautiful view.
She ordered a salad
but then wanted some pizza
off the plate of her partner.
But Partner
hunched over defiant
and clenched her cutlery
till her knuckles turned white
to prove they were bone.

I felt sad and thought back
to my own love affairs
that however tumultuous,
and dirty,
always involved sharing.
Joint sips from one coffee,
drags from the same smoke
until the inevitable divide.

MY EX HAD A BABY – with someone else

AND ITS BEEN YEARS SINCE
we've spoken –
and longer still since we've touched.

We always lived HEMISPHERES apart,
overcame foreign tongues and tastes –
back when we loved.

Times I HAVE ACHED for him.
Craved. But I recognise what I missed
as the illusion of intimacy,

and not the person who eluded me.
Still THE BABY rocks me. I don't know
its sex or name or birth weight.

I don't know the SCENT OF ITS CROWN-
ED newness or its niche
within its nuclear unit.

But I feel something CURLED INSIDE ME,
despite having children of my own,
grown big now. And I don't want

another. Never wanted his. Didn't want
him for long. But THE FACT OF A BABY.
The fact of him as Father,

WHEN I SAW him as a loner, a man
who wouldn't ever settle down.
It confounds rotation, yet keeps on turning,

however, stuck I feel.
That time with him LOOMS large for me,
but his time without me LOOMS larger.

Blame

The tornado furls, accelerates and whirls
around a lonely core of domestic violence.
The house entire lifts from its moorings.
Spins through slate skies. Plummets.
Lands upon that unfortunate witch. Killings
her instantly. And blowing havoc amongst
the munchkin population, who'd assumed
she was to blame.

And only now she's gone, do they begin
to ask those quantum questions
about whether this accident was accidental,
or the consequence of some malign force –
more potent than witchcraft. Her skinny
legs protrude in their grubby stockings. Kick
up clouds of bereavement. Only now –

do they regret her flimsy shelter.

Penetrate

1. I have a male friend who's impotent

When he apologises for not being able to fuck,
I don't answer any more –

just smile and ask for the bowl of chips to be
nudged closer.

I don't question him or me or vacillate or swing
on insecurities,

just cherish the rarefied safety on the eleventh floor.
The honesty of his apartment.

We share fast food and wine. I don't want sex either.
I don't bother saying why.

I wonder where virility resides, what impotence
inspires in me –

Imagine masculinity remoulded until it's new –
unarmoured and shiny.

After Adam Robert: 'Steven Returns the Universe', *Meanjin* Autumn 2022,* and Rachael Yehuda PhD et al. 'PTSD and Sexual Dysfunction in Men and Women', April 2015

* 'What would it look like for white masculinity to change? Would it have to die first?… It is easier to imagine apocalypse, our own end as a species, than to imagine a change in economic and political systems that would make other ways of being possible.'

2. His penis made me teary

(A dic pic ekphrastic)

Being single and female lends itself to unwanted dic pics. Instant deletions. Revulsions. Windswept plains of contempt for each organ that each one possesses. Each one believing each one to be rare. A hard-won triumph.

But then a different picture. The phone pings, and I startle. My towering builder friend. He's shrinking. Parental alienation, DV – gendered bias. He's sent me a black and white photograph of his flaccid penis. The following caption: *No sleaze intended* – and, indeed, none taken. The attached text: *A penis whipping system unbalanced by too much pussy whipping. This results in a new breed of male.* He is referencing the current dichotomy – domineering or emasculated. There seems to be no place, no grace, accorded to gentle men. The photo makes me cry, actually has me doubled over, hands on bended knees. I see vulnerability. Bravery. I also see a man who wouldn't – and now couldn't – commit rape. An unbalanced composition – of a politicised penis, which flops. Which penetrates.

Cleanliness is next to godliness – for some

1.

We shared a lovely breakfast. Creamy eggs Benedict
and good strong coffee. Afterwards, he scrubbed
the tabletop with a napkin – so I ended it there.
He asked for feedback as he worked concentric
circles, sweeping pittances into a pile. *It won't work*
I said not meaning to be rude. I walked it back –
It's because I'm messy – at best random. Trying
to amass the blame onto my own plate.
But when he rationalised, I changed tack. And tact.
Look, I've just decided –
I'll only date poets from now on. Which is untrue.

2.

IN THE month before inevitable
      separation, my father was staying
          over. Ducking domestic debris

of his own, he spilled all over ours.
      Oblivious, he enjoyed the home-
          cooked meals, the routine chaos

of children. Their endless demands
      for lifts and love. Weeks later,
          when it was over, the split split wide

and official, Dad surprised me
      with his perception. *I saw you vacuum*
          he said simply.

It was late. So I knew –

3.

You start in the centre and work
outwards – the dinner dishes or a general wipe.
It might fee cathartic to wash and hang laundry,
to wheel the bins out, to check the calendar,
and colour code. Scratch [or claw] beneath surfaces.
Maybe clear the fridge for clarity –
sort the still-edible from the dog-worthy.

Confront the pantry until it surrenders its chaos.
Clear cupboards and stuff bags for the Salvos.
Lean the ladder to reach the unreachables.
Subdue the lego with zip locks and air-
tight lids. [Is the tedium starting to drag at you yet?
Or are you still primed, still certain
you're just a spray away from a sparkling utopia?]

4.

It's good to breed delusions in place of germs
Note: if what you covet is hygiene,
attend to the instruments post-surgery.
When clotted blood and wet biomatter
cling fast to the forceps, scalpels and clamps.
When the only solution is toxic, wear gloves
when preparing the soak –
6 ml of Medizyme with clean water, 10 min.
Insure its bone dry before the autoclave 45-min cycle.
Then ask yourself, *Is this triumph?* Have you
completed the scour?

Totemism

The marriage counsellor
keeps a basket on her desk full
of plastic farm and zoo animals,
such as a child plays with. Sitting here,
I feel childlike and bestial. Both.
I reach. And my fingers close
around She-Wolf's neck. In that moment,
I know I divulge the secret, the one
camouflaged in broad daylight,
in lupine outrage, in long fangs behind
my smile and the matted grey coat I wear
beneath my faded denim jacket. I read
somewhere that when a wolf shows up
in a life, best to pay attention. And it shows
up in her basket, and in that core I'd call *soul,*
were that word still deemed worthy
of prowling into poems. I know my scent.
I pose no danger – less than my plastic double.
Unless hunted on my mountain top
or followed to my lair, you might take me
for tame. As long as my howl isn't stifled
or my fresh meat stolen, I unleash
a measure of civility. The room
ravages – and rocks. It recedes
along with the marriage counsellor,
her basket and my soon-to-be-ex.

Package deal

He was in my first post-separation batch.
I held him – a measure of promise up to the light.
Beautiful and brown. Hardly bigger than myself –
which suits someone not liking to be towered over,
dwarfed, or prevailed upon
by size, musculature – or other allied attributes.

All lacquered. His skin, teeth, hair compiled
a catalogue of self-containment. His parts moulded.
Melded. No far-flung limbs or words left trailing –
like my own. He travelled light. No weight-bowed
bones, or shoulders laden – no visible debris
in his crystalline wake. But he set me up

on the highest shelf, not dusty like some heavy
unread book, but fine like somene ornament –
admired, preserved, handled with infrequent finical care
in case overuse should chip, mar its sheen, deem it
devalued – or devastated. It took a year, for him to tell
me about the support group he attended,

then helped to run for those struggling
post-divorce – in bitterness, brokenness, or still in love.
It seems I never did have jurisdiction over trauma –
couldn't wrap it, dismember it, own it, or swallow it
whole. It won't cleave, drape, or fit me like a glove.
Freeing. One-size-fits-all.

Pattern making

After https://larivierefashion.com

The pattern is the foundation for the entire garment; pattern making is part creativity and part methodology. The blueprint.

1. Assemble your tools
2. Take measurements
3. Add style and design
4. Grade your concept
5. Move to draping

1. When you are four, it's easy for the big boy next door at Dad's to tack on a head job.
2. And when you are five, it's simple for the big boy next door at Mum's to grade you in the garden shed where it's dark and the cobwebs wrap greying rafters.
3. Then it's a basic step towards a GP who toiles you, all the while darting lewd sexual references at the bust line.
4. Which primes you for that dentist, that physio, that locksmith.
5. An entire block; row upon row of partners who have not yoked consent.

Settlement

I had never hoped to settle
down, but did. Married, and stayed inside

for decades. I apply no pressure to the swirl
of dust. And when the baby cries at night,

I'm patient, in sync with her noise – upheaval
is to be expected. I don't need it compacted

into sedimentary layers under my feet,
or in sheer cliff faces, picturesque in my middle

distance. I can writhe – and wrap
myself in swaths of time. The house can spin

when the wind picks up, when yellow notes slip
between fingers to careen past the bins, office

doors and court steps, loosening from paper files
and document towers because I don't aspire to pin

it down, to clamp, adhere or screw that vice. I live on.
Unimpeded. Unwaiting. And the property can settle

when and where it does, whatever the weather –
in due course. With or without orders.

Pure poet

I write one poem. I write another.
Then a ream. I write only for myself. Until –

I show a parent, a daughter, a friend. I meet a mentor.
A publisher. I get a particular response.

I write on. I redraft. Or I don't. I touch tall poppies.
Shake off short men. Start to win. I lose some

sympathy and support. All that amity –
I plummet from my writing group, where once

I havened. A lover loosens a poem from its post
upon my page. I lose a lover. I think I'll stop

showing the right work
to the wrong people

I build a thicker skin. A website.
A whole collection –

a manuscript. Stack volumes. I consider
radio, performance, bigger venues,

gloss journals, brighter outfits,
sponsorships, collaborations.

I spin nets and networks. I grow
audacious. And humble. Better

equipped for what it is
words do – to me.

The truth about my WRITING

I MAKE
SUBMISSIONS when I'm drunk.
I seldom do those final edits
or think through selections. Often
I don't remember what, or where

I've sent which work. I go
to a weekly writing workshop.
Sometimes I'm in love
with the work of peers.
Sometimes I grow bored,

carry on with my own poems
inside my head
or begin messaging the latest
person(s) I'm sleeping with
or wish to be. And I often lie

about how long I spent writing
this piece or that because I know
it's good.I know the others
will feel better if they think
it took me ages.

I so admire Medusa

I would so willingly hack
my long blonde strands –
switch them for living coils
of snakes in their stead.
Imagine the hissing halo.
Imagine the hell-bent nest.
The gazes
I could avert. And warp.
Imagine my stoicism
fixed beneath the wrath
of red kinetic tongues
limblessly
anchored down.
Reliant upon my skull.
Imagine my clear path.
As I shop aisles at Coles,
As I walk past construction
sites to silence. My peace.
My long panorama.

Cup of grit

Excuse the cliché at the start of a poem
But sometimes it simply is the simple things
And acts and if those acts involve warmth
Well then   see how I'm rising on the heat of this
From a cup of tea   a particular cup of tea at table
To pause   a frenetic day when nothing lifted
When I was cold despite my coat
Hungry despite my lunch
Lonely despite my love
Then the gentle push into my kitchen chair
Milky tea set before me
I hadn't requested   hadn't known I wanted
That arrived in an oversized mug   a bowl in fact
The way a hot drink is served in Paris
The way it's meant to scorch on its passage down
Once drained   I was flushed
Swilling steam in my throat
Grit and all until
Only cold dregs remained

The resurrection of the black banana

Listless in her fruit bowl.
Beyond bread making or even the blender.
Bent and humiliated.
Oozing her sweet custard,
she sprouts spores of blue-grey fuzz.

But following
a rare reversal, the crank of roll-back,
Xanthe willingly seeps back into skin.
As sunlight into morning.

Despite quantities of ethylene, the proximity of apples,
and the passing of fruitful time, this banana persists.
Eventually a greenness tinges the leathery peel –
and the fruit grows firm.

She's all fragrant farewell.
Via string bags and car boot to the grocery store.
In a sturdy packing crate, she enjoys the community vibe
of stacked pallets in the back of a refrigerated HGV.
A full day later, I am notified of her safe arrival.

To her, most gratifying is her decision
to rejoin a part-cluster.
She reclines against the plastic liner,
enjoying the banter on both sides of the slip sheet.
No fear of blackening here – on an absorbent paper floor.
Feeling the pump and flow of cool cool cool air.

Upon arrival in the Tully region of northern Queensland,
even an icy bath cannot subdue her.
At the packing shed, the bunch cover is replaced.
Huddled on a padded trailer, she's upright.
She changes her name to Cavendish.

They drive.
Back to the fields.
Back to the plants.
Back to the stems.
In the tropical heat heat heat.

The hawk and the tripper

I told him I liked tattoos
      and he showed me the hawk
spread-eagled across his chest

in thick oceans of bluest ink
      which led me to contemplate
otherness – like wolves

and dogs and open ground
      because I love to tramp
along clifftops and view

the wildest blue below
      beyond and above us all
and spumes of other colours

that I see and seek to wear
      depending on my mood my time
and what isn't in the washing pile

Assertive

amateur at conflict
I hedge and shirk
dodge
the waves
that merge to menace
in high-rise rollers
rips and breakers
that wash   and wish
I had spoken up
on shore

Dragons don't smoke

    I draw a cruel lungful of fresh air. And let go.
A whooooooooooshh sounds. With scales iridescent
I unlatch my great jaws. This time words pour forth
and bounce between cliff walls – my meaning is hot,
unwavering and still. I watch as its glowing end
    smoulders and shrinks. The sudden clarity –
no cigarette lasts forever. As barriers go, too flimsy
to install between fears and their sources. As far as
procrastination – when craving eons, mere minutes

spill madly as that most notorious milk. I could soon
be cramped again – in that dank lair, behind boulders.
In airlessness. So, after packets, entire cartons smoked
to ash, I put this out half smoked. And grind it under
a yellowing claw. I exhale like the dragon I've always
wanted to love – purple plumes shoot from my mouth
to rival the stratosphere. I watch as my dense breaths
    mingle with storm clouds. I watch until smoke
and vapour merge. I watch until there's no distinction

    between that of my lungs, and that of the sky.

Acknowledgements

'Dementia is preferable' – *Fish Anthology* 2023
'Paddington Bear' – *Victorian Writers* 2023
'The Hurricane' – Baltimore Science Fiction and Fantasy Contest 2002
'I so admire Medusa' – *The Canberra Times* 2022
'Dragons don't smoke' – *Minds Shine Bright Anthology* 2022
'The beginning of love is hardly the challenge' and 'The sharing of love' – *Poetry d'Amour Contest Anthology* 2022
'The word ecosystem seeped into my head' – Gem Zines 2022
'Between', 'Old One Eye', 'In Public' and 'Comfort zone' – *Australian Catholic University Anthology* 2022
'Pattern making' – *Cordite* 106: *OPEN* 2022
'The hawk and the tripper' – Melbourne Poets Union Prize 2021
'Sober hook up' – *Slush Love* 2021
'The resurrection of the black banana' and 'Cup of grit' – *Australian Catholic University Anthology* 2021

www.ingramcontent.com/pod-product-compliance
Lightning Source LLC
Chambersburg PA
CBHW071036080526
44587CB00015B/2637